Table of Contents:

Introduction:

Reasoning Skills is a homework program designed to help your clients get what you want in ways that do not later cause then (and others) problems. It is easy to do. Have your client read one lesson at a time. Each lesson asks them questions which they write their answers on a piece of paper that they supply.

If reading or writing are not their strong areas, you can let them use a friend or family member to help. They then turn their paper in the next time you meet with them. You can write comments on their paper and return it to them later. Use a pen for your comments, so they stand out. It is better to us a color other than red, because it carries connotations of failure. It is also good to discuss some of their answers with them as well. It provides an opportunity to do some counseling.

You will tell them how often a lesson is to be turned in. Keep in mind you may run the program differently to suit you specific needs.

Reasoning Skills will help increase your clients' thinking skills by showing ways to manage their emotions and effectively solve problems. The better they becoming in getting things that they value, the less they are likely to make legal choices and choices that are freer from conflict.

About the Author:

Russ Fry retired December 31, 2007 after 33 years of service with the 8th Iowa Judicial District Department of Correctional Services. He worked as a probation officer, residential counselor and for the last 13 years as a Community Treatment Coordinator specializing in cognitive-behavioral interventions. He developed and facilitated curriculums for offenders who were not ready for treatment, as well as conducted training for the State of Iowa in cognitive-behavioral interventions and discovery/experiential-based facilitator skills.

Russ now presents trainings to correctional departments and other human service providers. His topics cover all of the principles discussed in these articles and more

Russ was on the 2006/2008 board of the Iowa Corrections Association and was the recipient of the 2006 Iowa Corrections Association's Outstanding Correctional Worker's award. He was also named 2007 Employee of the Year for the 8th Iowa Judicial District Department of Correctional Services.

Russ has a BA from the University of Northern Iowa and an MA in Liberal Studies (with an emphasis in Psychology) from Excelsior College in Albany, New York. He has taught for St. Ambrose University and Southeastern Community College.

Some of the areas Russ has been trained in are: Motivational Interviewing, Foundation Skills for Trainers, Managing Offenders with Psychological Disorders, Brief Cognitive Applications for Everyday Offender Management, Criminal Conduct and Substance Abuse Treatment, How People Change: Applying the Trans-theoretical Model, Cognitive/Behavioral Strategies, Impact of Crime on Victims, Sex Offender Treatment, Cognitive Approaches to Changing Offender Behavior, A Framework for Breaking Barriers, Positive Solutions and Reasoning and Rehabilitation.

Russ lives in Burlington, Iowa with his wife Connie and can be reached at 12434 Y-Camp Rd., Burlington, Iowa 52601, (319)750-4411 or rfry52601@aol.com.

REASONING SKILLS
SCORING GUIDE

01. What Does It Mean to Have a Problem (To have the students think about whether they need to develop knowledge, skills resources or motivation in order to fix one of their problem areas)

    1. Write a definition of the word *problem* just like you were writing it for a dictionary.

        (Any honest answer will do - usually an obstacle or a mystery.)

    2. Answer this question yes or no: Does this man have a problem by your definition? Explain your answer

        (Any honest answer will do.)

    3. Does that change your mind about whether he has a problem or not? Explain your answer.

        (Any honest answer will do.)

    4. Write what a person needs to develop if they want to pilot a plane.

        (Knowledge, skills and resources – however, most people give concrete examples of these answers.)

    5. Write Yes or No to this question: Can everyone develop the ability to pilot a plane? Explain your answer.

        (No, some people do not have the potential. For example, it is unlikely that a person who is blind and quadriplegic could not develop the ability to fly a plane.)

    6. Write Yes or No to this question: Does everyone with the ability to do something - do it? Explain your answer.

        (No. Some people just are not motivated to do it)

    7. Write a paragraph about what the guy in the movie is missing in order to get and stay sober – capacity, motivation or ability - and why you think that.

        (Any honest answer will do.)

    8. Think of one of your problems. Write down what that problem is and then write a paragraph about what area – capacity, motivation or ability – do you think you need to work on - and why you think that.

        (Any honest answer will do.)

02. Accident (To explore the situations in which we get angry and how our responses to those situations cannot be considered an accident)

    1. Write down 5 things that make you mad.

        (Any honest answers will do.)

    2. 1B, 2D, 3E, 4C, 5A

    3. Most people rank culpability this way: 1 Accident, 2 Lack of Knowledge and Skills, 3 Careless, 4 Reckless and 5 Deliberate

    4. Write how you think you would feel if someone cut in front of you like that.

        (Any honest answer will do.)

    5. Write what you might think about the person who cut in front of you.

        (Any honest answer will do.)

    6. Write what you might do in response.

4

(Any honest answer will do.)
7.   1D, 2A, 3E, 4B, 5C
8. Write about what you see as the disadvantages of acting before you know what is really going on when you are angry about something (like someone cutting in line in front of you).
   (You might create problems for yourself or others when it could have been avoided. Any honest answer will do.)
9. Write the letter of the reason listed below for the way you acted the last time you got real angry at someone - and did something you regretted later: **A)** ACCIDENT, B) CARELESS, C) RECKLESS, D) LACKING KNOWLEDGE AND SKILLS, E) DELIBERATE
   (Any honest answer will do.)
10. Write a sentence or two about why you think you responded that way. What were your thoughts about the person?
   (Any honest answer will do.)
11. Write a sentence or two about why losing your temper is not an accident, if you know the kind of stuff that makes you mad or act before you know what is really going on.
   (An accident is unforeseeable or unavoidable. If you know what kinds of things make you angry you can prepare yourself so that you do not lose your temper. In other words, it is foreseeable and alterable. Any honest answer will do.)
12. Write whether you think avoiding problems is a matter of will power or whether a person also needs knowledge and skills. Explain your answer.
   (Will power is largely motivation. You also need knowledge - what are your triggers - and skills - how to manage emotions, problem solving and so on.)
13. Pick 3 of the following knowledge and skills that you think would help you the most with keeping out of trouble in the future. Write their numbers down and explain why you think they would help.
   1. Understanding the differences between people.
   2. Knowing my triggers (things that I get angry about).
   3. Knowing ways to manage my emotions.
   4. Knowing when I am getting worked up before I do anything I'll regret later.
   5. Knowing how to calm down.
   6. Knowing how to deal with stress.
   7. How to set goals.
   8. Having a clear idea about what is important to me.
   9. Keeping in mind those things that are important to me so that I don't do anything to harm them.
   10. How to solve problems without making more problems later.
   11. How to let go of things that I want, but cannot have.
   12. How to communicate well enough so that other people really understand me.
   13. How to stop blaming other people for things I do.
   14. Changing beliefs that seem right, but that get me into trouble.
   15. How to stick to my plans and not get sidetracked.
   16. How to keep from doing stupid things because of alcohol or other drugs.
   17. How to relax.
   (Any honest choices will do.)

03. Two Mind (To discuss how we sometimes make emotional decisions and sometimes make rational decisions)
   1R, 2E, 3E, 4E, 5R, 6E, 7R, 8R, 9E, 10R, 11E, 12E, 13R, 14R

15. Write a sentence or two on what you think each of these techniques are and how
they might help eliminate dysreasoning effects.

Value clarification helps you know in a mindful way what is important to
you. It helps you act according to your priorities.

Refuting irrational ideas helps you get rid of ideas that cause you problems.

Management of emotions is a skill to keep calm and think clearly.

Problem solving is a skill that figure out what to do when you have a
problem.

Relaxation training teaches you techniques on how to calm down. When you
are calm, you can think clearer.

Recognizing problem areas and response rehearsal are trainings on
knowing in a mindful way what types of situations cause you problems and
then practice how you are going to respond in those ways. If you act a lot
without thinking, these techniques help you respond to problem areas in an
automatic way that you have chosen.

16. Write a sentence or two on which of these techniques you think would be most
useful for you to use more often and why.

(Any honest answer will do.)

04. Values (To think about what is important to us and how we respond when things do
not go our way)

1 to 10. List 10 things you value. Then add a $ sign in front of those things that cost
money, an A in front of those things you like to do alone, an O if front of things you
like to do with others, a P in front of those things that require planning and an L in
front of things that will be on your list for some time. Then circle the 3 most
important. Then, if none of them are for other people's benefit, add a couple that are.

11. List 3 other examples of unrealistic wants.

(Any honest answer will do.)

12. List 3 other examples of incompatible haves and wants.

(Any honest answer will do.)

13. Are any of the items on your list unrealistic? Are there things on your list that are
incompatible with other more important things? Explain why you think that way.

(Any honest answer will do.)

14. Write how you feel when your overall haves and wants match you getting and
keeping? Or, in other words, when you are doing a good job at getting what you
want.

(Happy, fulfilled, power, control elation, pleasure, satisfaction, joy or any
other positive emotions)

15. Write how you feel when you are not doing a good job at getting what you want.

(Unfulfilled, discontented, angry, sad, worried, fearful or any other negative
emotion)

16. Sometimes people don't get what they want because they let their emotions get in
the way. An example, you want a job but get mad at the interviewer and call him
an idiot when he questions you about something on your application. List 3 other
examples of not getting what you want because of emotions.

(Any honest answer will do.)

17. Are there things on it that you are not getting because of the way you go about trying to get them? If so, which things? Is that because you are careless (not paying enough attention), reckless (taking too many chances), don't know how to get what you want without creating other problems, too impulsive, alcohol or other drugs use is interfering with clear thinking, because of poor problem solving skills, or some other reason? Why do you think this is so?

    (Any honest answer will do.)

18. People often Muddle-through rather than problem solve or cope. For example, go drinking when you have a fight with you partner. List 3 examples of muddle-through.

    (Any honest answer will do.)

19. Why you think people sometimes muddle-through rather than problem solve or cope?

    (They may feel it is easier to do nothing. they may just hope things will get better on their own. Any honest answer will do.)

20. List 3 examples of people using a phantom fix.

    (Use alcohol or other drugs, overeat, compulsive shopping or gambling, kick the dog or yell at the kids to feel powerful and in control.)

21. 1E, 2C, 3F, 4B, 5A, 6D

22. Write one of things you value that you are not currently getting? Then write how that makes you feel. Write what you think about not getting it? Then write how you are dealing with it: Problem Solving, Coping, Muddling-through – Blaming, Muddling-through – Avoidance Strategies, Phantom Fix, Power Fix.

    (Any honest answer will do.)

05. Taming Your Beast (To learn how to keep your emotions under control)

1. Write down 25 emotions. Then write a plus sign (+) behind each emotion that makes you feel good and a minus sign (-) behind each emotion that makes you feel bad. Then get another piece of paper and make a chart like this on it. Then go through your list of emotions, pick out the negative emotions and write them on your chart next to emotions to which they are most closely related. For example, rage would probably go next to anger and grief would probably go next to sadness.

2. Answer these questions:

    Why did he bring her the flowers?

    (He probably felt bad about what he had done.)

    What emotion do you think he was experiencing when he was hitting her?

    (Anger, rage – maybe power and control.)

    If he was angry, what might he have thought was a threat to him?

    (He might have thought that she was cheating on him. That he would lose her. Any honest answer will do.)

    What advantage might hitting her offer him?

    (She might do what he wants her to do.)

    What disadvantage might that behavior cause him?

    (She might leave him. He might go to jail. Any honest answer will do.)

Do you think his behavior got him what he wanted - in the short run? Explain your answer.

> (Any honest answer will do. Maybe it did.)

Do you think his behavior will get him what he wants - in the long run? Explain your answer.

> (Probably not. Any honest answer will do.)

3. Think about a time when you experienced emotions so strong that you did something that you regretted later. Who were you with? What time was it? Was it day or night? Were you inside or out? Were you warm or cold? Were there any sounds in the background? Write a paragraph about that incident. Then imagine how it might have turned out had you approached it with positive thoughts and positive emotions. Rewrite the story how it would have happened if you had slowed down and problem solved before you acted.

06. Space Villain vs. Robert E. Lee (Understanding the dangers of being seduced by the emotions of power and control)

1. There is an old adage that you can get a donkey to do what you want with a carrot or a stick. Write what you think that adage means?

> (Any honest answer will do. You can get others to do what you want through intimidation or encouragement.)

2. Why Darth Vader choked the man? Do you think that everyone else was intimidated by Darth Vader and the Dark Side of the Force? Will they all be less likely to cross Darth Vader in the Future?

> (He chocker the man to intimidate him and others, so that they would do what he wanted them to do.)

3. Write a sentence or two about someone that treated you that way.

> (Any honest answer will do.)

4. In the *Return of the Jedi* Luke Skywalker was captured by Darth Vader and the Emperor was going to seduce him to the Dark Side. Do you remember how that was to happen? Write your answer.

> (He was going to get Luke very angry and get him to feel the power that comes from it. This would turn him to the dark side.)

5. Pick the three neutralizing thoughts that you believe cause the most harm. Then write why you picked them

> Moral Justification
> Euphemistic Language
> Advantageous Comparison
> Displacement of Responsibility
> Diffusion of Responsibility
> Distorting Consequences
> Attribution of Blame
> Dehumanization
> (Any honest answer will do.)

6. Write of your experience when someone helped you when you made a mistake rather than treated you badly.

> (Any honest answer will do.)

07. Problem Solving (To learn how to systematically solve problems without your emotional mind getting in the way)

1. Write how you know when you have a problem.

   (You feel angry, sad, worried or afraid.)

2. Write what the problem is.

   (How is he going to get to the interview on time?)

3. List the differences.

   (*Picture on left*: 1) arrow on upper left points up, 2) triangle near lightning in upper center missing, 3) arrows in lines on upper right is in the middle, 4) lasso with loop in middle has a dot in it, 5) arrow to right of lasso loop is longer, 6) the *N* in *and* is capitalized, 7) hourglass on lower left is smaller, 8) oval in block on lower left is on left side of block, 9) arrow pointing to oval in center bottom is missing, 10) oval above *think* is horizontal, 11) box with arrow, at the top center, has a thinner boarder.)

4. Melissa's dead naked body lay on the floor. She is in a puddle of water. The window is open and the breeze is blowing the curtains about. There is broken glass everywhere. What happened to Melissa? Write what questions you would ask to get the answer.

   (Most people just make guesses about what happened.)

5. What are the specific types of questions reporters are taught to ask (if you don't know – write *don't know*)?

   (Who, what, where, when, why and how type questions)

6. Write down some: who, what, where, when, why and how questions that – if answered – would tell the story of this newspaper article about a man arrested with 141 pounds of pot.

   (What was his name? How old was he. Where did he live? Where was he going? Where was he arrested? Who arrested him? How did they find the pot? Why did they stop him? What was he charged with? What are the penalties if he is convicted?)

7. What are the facts of the schoolyard fight story?

   (A teacher sees two kids fighting in the schoolyard. One is black and one is white.)

8. What are the facts in the picture?

   (The man on the left has a prosthesis (an artificial arm).

   He is black. Is he an African American? We don't know he could be French.

   He is wearing an Army shirt. Was he in the Army? We don't know. Anyone can buy a used army shirt.

   Is his name Franks? We don't know for the same reason.

   The little black girl is holding his hand. What is their relationship? We don't know. He could be her father, brother or even baby sitter.

   She is wearing bibs.

   There is a little girl in the lower right hand corner holding a doll.

   The older man has glasses on. Is he old? Old is relative.

   He has what some call on overseas cap on. Was he in the military? We don't know.

He has a bow tie and a jacket on.

Are the two men saluting? This is real technical, but we don't know. To salute you have to be saluting at something and we cannot see that they are. The best we can say is that they have their hands to their forehead in a saluting position.

Are they at parade? We don't know.

There is a lawn chair behind the black girl.

The number 8 and balloons behind the older man.)

9. What would you order from the pizza menu?

    (Any honest answer will do.)

10. List 15 names of some family members, friends and acquaintances.

    (Any honest answer will do.)

11. List several brainstorming ideas about how the guy can get to the interview on time.

    (Any honest answer will do.)

12. Write 5 reasons marijuana should be legalized and 5 reasons why it should not. The idea is to think about both sides of the issue (whether you agree with the other side or not)

    (Any honest answer will do.)

13. Write about something that happened in your life that would have turned out better if you had done just a little of this problem solving first – before you acted.

    (Any honest answer will do.)

08. Being Responsible (To discuss the negative consequences of blaming fate, our nature or the way we were raised for the problems we create for ourselves)

1. Answer whether you think there really was a flood, locusts and earthquakes? Or did John Belushi's character just say those things to get out of a jam?

    (He is just trying to get out of a jam)

2. Write how you think it hurts a person, in the long run, when they knowingly make excuses for things they have done that hurt other people?

    (They do not try to change and continue to hurt people. this creates enemies who not only will not help them in times of trouble, but will also go out of their way to cause them problems.)

3. Write what this is a picture of.

    (An old woman)

4. Write what this is a picture of.

    (Some will say an old woman. Others will say a young woman)

5. Match the picture with the definition.

    (Fate – safe falling on guy, Nature – car wreck and Nurture – old/young woman)

6. Which of these are fate?

    a. My parents were alcoholics.

    b. I go drinking every Friday and Saturday night.

    c. I smoke pot every chance I get.

    d. My dad used to beat me.

e. I am on probation.

f. I have a good job.

g. I have a bad job.

h. I hang out in bars

(a, d – one might make a case for f and g claiming they were all that were available.)

7. List at least 5 things that happened to you that were just fate - 5 things that you do just because of your nature – in other words, because you like to do those things - and 5 things that you do because you were brought up that way.

(Any honest answer will do.)

8. Think about the act that you did that got you in trouble. Was it fate that you did it, your nature that you did it or the way you were brought up that cause you to do it?

(Any honest answer will do.)

9. Think about whether a person can choose to act differently from the way that they like to act or can act differently than they way they were brought up. Can they sometimes overcome fate? Write your thoughts on the paper.

(Yes. Any honest answer will do.)

10. Write how it hurts a person, in the long run, if they blame their fate in life, they way they were raised or their nature for the harm they cause others – rather than problem solve (fix things) or cope (accept what they cannot change)?

(They never make to effort to make their life better.)

11. What happens to a person if they tell themselves that they cannot change?

(Their life never gets better and probably gets worse.)

09. Callous Heart (To help students see the connection between callous thoughts and the harm they cause to others and to the thinker of those thoughts)

1. What emotion do you think the motel manager was experiencing? Did he have to help her? Why did he want to take care of her?

(He probably felt sorry for her. No. Because she needed help.)

2. What emotion you think the German officer might have been feeling?

(None – no emotion)

Make an Empathy/Indifference Chart and put where you think you are on it.

EMPATHY (feeling for others)

1.
2.
3.
4.
5.
6.
7.
8.
9.
10.

INDIFFERENCE (lack of empathy)

(Any honest answer will do.)

3. Have you ever did hard work with your hands? Did you ever develop calluses? What are calluses?

(Calluses are thickening of the skin where there is frequent friction. They protect the skin from pain and further damage. Any honest answer will do.)

4. Do you think the German officer was always so cold blooded?

(No.)

Do you think that long before the war he loved, laughed, cared for other people and had other people who truly cared for him?

(Probably.)

Before the war, do you think he might have been horrified if he had seen someone shot before his eyes?

(Probably.)

5. How does someone go from a decent person – like the manager at the hotel - to one who is so uncaring, so callous, and so indifferent to someone else's suffering?

(When they first do something that hurts other people, they feel bad, but if they make up excuses that justifies in their minds that it was ok, they do not feel so bad any more.)

6. Pick the five excuses that you think have allowed the worst things to happen in the world.

1. They deserved it.
2. No one was really hurt that much anyway.
3. She's making too big a deal over this.
4. It's a tough world and I ain't any worse than anyone else.
5. It ain't my fault.
6. I was high.
7. I was just teaching her about sex.
8. They made me mad.
9. I didn't have a choice.
10. I really did them a favor.
11. If I hadn't done it, someone else would have.
12. They knew better than to do that to me
13. It's a stupid law anyway.
14. Everyone else is doing it.
15. I didn't really want that to happen.
16. I was drunk.
17. They've got insurance, so no one was hurt.
18. Everyone is really crooked anyway.
19. I'm no worse than anyone else.
20. They screwed me, I screwed them back.
21. I don't want to think about it.
22. Screw everybody.
23. (Your idea)__________________.
24. (Your idea)__________________.

(Any honest choices will do.)

Write the excuses that you have used before on the left side of your other paper, the one with *empathy* on the top and *indifference* on the bottom. Then look at the "indifferent thoughts" that you wrote on the left side of your other paper, the one with *empathy* on the top and *indifference* on the bottom. Re-write those thoughts (on the right side of the paper) so that it makes you more sensitive to other people's feelings – that aren't excuses – that holds yourself accountable for what you do but also keep you from getting a callous heart.

(Any honest answer will do.)

7. Write the advantages of not thinking callous thoughts
(You don't become indifferent to other people's pain. You are less likely to hurt other people. You don't lose touch with your own empathy. You don't lose you ability to feel good. Any honest answer will do.)

10. The Cost of Living With Crime (To show them that the harm done by a criminal act goes far beyond the act itself)

1. Write $1000 and draw a car or truck next to the number. Your vehicle will also be worth $1000.

2. Pick your insurance policy (a) No Insurance, (b) $200 deductible, (c) Full coverage. Write the letter doe the policy. Then subtract the cost of that policy from your $1000 and write the answer on your paper.

3. Write the letter A or B or C or D.

4. Write how much money you have left after taking care of this.

5. These are things that happen in neighborhoods because of crime:

1. Victims might emotionally struggle to figure out why it happened to them.
2. Victims may find it difficult to trust anyone again.
3. Victims may have to buy more insurance.
4. Victims may have to depend upon others for rides and feel like they are a burden on their friends.
5. Victims might isolate themselves - stay inside all the time.
6. Victims might be late for school or work or lose work time and wages.
7. Victims may have to pay medical costs.
8. Victims may have trouble sleeping.
9. Victims may blame themselves and be embarrassed.
10. Victims may have to pay for losses out of their own pocket.
11. Victims may be very angry or sad or worried or afraid.
12. Victims may pay insurance deductibles or have their insurance rates go up.
13. Victims and all other tax payers may have their taxes go up because of the need for more law enforcement and prisons.
14. Victims may lose personal items that cannot be replaced
15. Victims may have to walk
16. Victims may feel powerless.
17. Victims might have to move.
18. Victims may have to clean up after vandalism

Write the things that you might experience if you were a victim of this type of vandalism. Next to each write a little about why you think that you might experience such things.
(Any hones answers will do.)

6. Even if you had no damage done during an incident of vandalism in your neighborhood, how might it affect you anyway? Explain your thoughts on this.
(Neighbors might need rides. You might be afraid it could happen to you. You insurance might go up. Taxes might go up. Any hones answers will do.)

7. Pick your insurance policy (a) No Insurance, (b) $200 deductible, (c) Full coverage. Write the letter doe the policy. Then subtract the cost of that policy from your $1000 and write the answer on your paper.
8. Write the letter A or B or C or D.
9. Write how much money you have left after taking care of this. If you have to borrow money write how much you had to borrow (along with the words "I had to borrow).
10. Subtract the money you have left from $1000. (If you had to borrow money, add the money you borrowed to you answer). Then divide your answer by 8. Write your answer. Also, write what you might do if you actually had that much extra money right now.
    (Any honest answer will do.)
11. Write how much money do you think most people would pay for theft and vandalism insurance if no one ever stole or vandalized cars?
    (Probably none for vandalism policies.)
12. Might there be some people who are afraid to go out after dark because of crime? Who might they be? Are their fears justified? Are they still afraid whether their fears are justified or not? Write your answers and explain them.
    (Yes. Maybe the elderly. Children. It doesn't matter. They are still afraid.)
13. Write what you think victims feel about people who harm them or their property. Why do they feel that way? Write your answers and explain them.
    (They are often angry. People shouldn't do things that harm others. Any honest answer will do.)
14. Write how a crime can turn violent even when the person committing it does not intend before hand for that to happen?
    (Maybe the victim would catch the vandals in the act and shoot them. Or the vandals might shoo the victim. Any honest answer will do.)
15. Pick your insurance policy (a) No Insurance, (b) $200 deductible, (c) Full coverage. Write the letter doe the policy. Then subtract the cost of that policy from your $1000 and write the answer on your paper.
16. Write the letter A or B or C or D.
17. Write how much money you have left after taking care of this. If you have to borrow money write how much you had to borrow (along with the words "I had to borrow).
18. How would you feel, after all of this you got a phone call and found out that you were fired for missing too much work? Or, evicted for missing payments? Or, have people thinking you did something wrong to have all this happen to you? This is what they mean by revictimization. Write how you would feel.
    (It makes people feel real bad. They could easily become depressed.)
19. What would you tell the judge about your experience? What all happened to you? How do you feel? What do you think the judge should do to the vandal?
    (Any honest answer will do.)
20. Write what the victim of your current offense would tell the judge about their experience. What all happened to them? How do they feel? What they think the judge should do to you. Remember, even if you had no specific victim, we have seen how crime can affect everyone in the community. If your crime did

not have a specific victim, write instead how what you did caused your
community to be a worse place to live.
(Any honest answer will do.)

11. Being Part of a System (To show students that being part of a system contributes its
negative consequences even if one does not directly participate in the negative aspects
themselves)
1. What do you call the effect when you line up a bunch of dominos and push the
end one over and they each fall in turn?
(The Domino Effect.)
2. List 10 people that are needed to keep a city bus system going.
(Riders, bus drivers, mechanics, administrators, payroll staff, accountants,
secretaries, janitors, receptionists, building maintenance, advertisers, etc)
3. What would happen to the domino effect if one or two dominos were removed
from the middle?
(The dominos would only fall as far as the gap and then stop.)
4. Would the bus system eventually come to a halt if there were NO bus drivers,
mechanics, secretaries, administrators, accountants, purchasing agents,
foreman, or janitors? How about riders? Would the system eventually come to
a halt if there were NO riders?
(Yes)
5. Answer these questions:
A. Is the guy who sold the gun part of a system? Explain why you think
this.
(Yes. He is part of how some crimes gets done. If there were no
one doing what he does, the system wouldn't function.)
B. How might the guy who sold the gun feel about what happened to the
victims of the robbery?
(Probably not anything. If he felt bad, he couldn't keep doing what
he does.)
C. How might the people who were robbed at gunpoint feel about the
robber?
(Angry)
D. How might the people who were robbed at gunpoint feel about the guy
who sold the illegal gun?
(Just as angry.)
Do you think that their feelings are justified (the seller didn't actually
commit the robbery)?
(Yes. If there were no one doing what he does, the chances of a
robbery would diminish.)
E. Looking at it from a systems perspective, how does a different customer
of illegal guns (who didn't participate in the robbery) contribute to the
robbery?
(If there were no one buying illegal guns, there would be no one
selling illegal guns and the number of robberies would drop.)
6. Answer these questions:

A. How might the guy who sold the gun feel about what happened to the victims and their families?

> (Maybe sad. Maybe afraid he might get caught, because the police will really be looking into this crime. However, if he felt bad, he couldn't keep doing what he does.)

B. How might the parents of the dead children feel about the killer?

> (Very revengeful. Any other honest answer will do.)

C. How might the parents of the dead children feel about the guy who sold the illegal gun?

> (Just as angry.)

Do you think that their feelings are justified (the seller didn't actually pull the trigger)?

> (Yes. He is part of the system that helps things like this to happen.)

D. How might the guy who sold the illegal gun feel if one of the children killed was his little sister?

> (Any honest answer will do.)

E. Looking at it from a systems perspective, how does a different customer of illegal guns (who didn't participate in the shootings) contribute to the shootings?

> (He is part of the system that helps things like this to happen.)

7. Answer these questions:

A. How do you think the mother felt about leaving her baby in the trash?

> (Probably upset. But at the time, her real concern was getting high.)

B. Do you think she planned to have harm come to her son? What do you believe she was thinking?

> (She probably didn't intend any harm coming to him. She was probably thinking something like, "He'll be safe here. I'll be right back. Everything will be ok.")

C. Was her son harmed regardless of what she intended?

> (Yes.)

D. Is the harm done to victims less injurious because the people who harm them did not intent to do so?

> (No.)

8. Answer these questions:

A. The male doctor asked the social worker to "sign off" on Isaiah. He was asking her to just let the baby die. What do you think about the doctor?

> (Any honest answer will do.)

B. Why do you think he was so callous, so heartless?

> (He had seen too much bad things and he tried not to feel bad anymore by no longer caring.)

C. Do you think he was always so cold hearted?

> (No. Most doctors go into the profession to help people.)

D. What might he have told himself that made it less hurtful to him that the baby should be allowed to die?

("I didn't put the baby in the trash. He'll only have a screwed up life anyway. He's better off dead." Any honest answer will do.)
E. How do you think finding a baby in the trash affected the garbage men?
(It probably traumatized them. They would probably double check all the trash for some time to come.)
F. How do you think a newspaper story about a baby in the trash affected the readers?
(Usually, people get upset.)
G. Do you think this kind of stuff leads to stricter laws or laws creating more treatment centers?
(Some people want to lock drug people up and throw away the key. Others think they need help.)

9. Who paid for the ambulance ride? Who paid the doctor bills? Who paid the hospital bills?
(Taxpayers. Or the hospitals tack the extra expenses to their costs – which then pass on to their customers – which then causes insurance rates to go up.)

10. Do you think illegal drugs have a system to support them? Explain your answer.
(Yes. There are many people with different jobs. Many of which, if no one did, the system would come to a halt.)

11. List of all of the people necessary to keep the illegal drug system going.
(Growers, manufactures, smugglers, mules, dealers, and users. Any other honest answer will do.)

12. Answer these questions:
A. Looking at it from a systems perspective, how does the person who sold illegal drugs to Isaiah's mother contribute to the Isaiah being put in the trash?
(He or she is part of a system. Their part contributes to keeping the system going.)
B. Looking at it from a systems perspective, how does another user contribute to the Isaiah being put in the trash?
(He or she is part of a system. Their part contributes to keeping the system going.)
C. How is a person who is part of a drug system, but denies contributing to the negative outcomes (like Isaiah being put in the trash) similar to the illegal gun dealer or the" sign off" doctor?
(They probably originally felt badly about the harm they do, but they talked themselves out of feeling bad. Eventually, they became calloused about all the harm they contributed to. They could hurt people and not care.)

13. What is the disadvantage of becoming a person who contributes to the harming of others and not feel bad about it?
(You can go from being a good person to one who can hurt people without caring. You become worse and the people around you suffer.)

12. Finding Your Way (To discuss what the student's life goals are, what they need to do to get them and what the obstacles are)

1. Imagine a friend called you on the phone and asked for directions – she wanted you to make her a map. What three things would you need to know in order to make her the map?

   (Where she is at, where she is going and the directions.)

   Make a map from your home to one of your favorite places. Make lined for the streets you will use. Make sure you label the streets.

2. Look at your map. Find the first major intersection. If you went the wrong way at that intersection, what would be something that you would see that made you say, "Hey – I'm going the wrong way"? Write that down.

   (Any honest answer will do.)

3. If you walked into a home in which the husband and wife didn't get along. What would you see and hear that let you know that that was the case? How do people feel when they are not getting along? What might be some of their thoughts?

   (Any honest answer will do.)

4. If you walked into a home in which the residents were unemployed. What would you see and hear that let you know that that was the case? How do people feel when they are not working? What might be some of their thoughts?

   (Any honest answer will do.)

5. If you walked into a home in which one of the residents was sick. What would you see and hear that let you know that that was the case? How do people feel when they are sick? What might be some of their thoughts?

   (Any honest answer will do.)

6. If you walked into a home in which one of the residents had low self-esteem. What would you see and hear that let you know that that was the case? How do people feel when they have low self-esteem? What might be some of their thoughts?

   (Any honest answer will do.)

7. If you walked into a home in which residents used alcohol or other drugs. They **did not** consider it a problem. What would you see and hear that let you know that that was the case? How do people feel when they have low self-esteem? What might be some of their thoughts?

   (Any honest answer will do.)

8. If you walked into a home in which residents used alcohol or other drugs. They **did** consider it a problem. What would you see and hear that let you know that that was the case? How do people feel when they have low self-esteem? What might be some of their thoughts?

   (Any honest answer will do.)

9. Write your thoughts on how these are all related.

   (Any honest answer will do.)

10. Now you walked into a home in which the husband and wife get along. What would you see and hear that let you know that that was the case? How do people feel when they are getting along? What might be some of their thoughts?

   (Any honest answer will do.)

11. If you walked into a home in which the residents were employed. What would
you see and hear that let you know that that was the case? How do people feel
when they are not working? What might be some of their thoughts?
    (Any honest answer will do.)
12. If you walked into a home in which the residents were healthy. What would
you see and hear that let you know that that was the case? How do people feel
when they are healthy? What might be some of their thoughts?
    (Any honest answer will do.)
13. If you walked into a home in which one of the residents had healthy self-
esteem. What would you see and hear that let you know that that was the case?
How do people feel when they have healthy self-esteem? What might be some
of their thoughts?
    (Any honest answer will do.)
14. If you walked into a home in which residents no longer use alcohol or other
drugs. What would you see and hear that let you know that that was the case?
How do people feel when they are in recovery? What might be some of their
thoughts?
    (Any honest answer will do.)
You know what your main problem area is like when it is bad. You know what
you want life to be like when your problem is fixed. Take the map you drew
earlier and put how that problem looks now on the bottom of the page - that is
where you are. You can draw a picture or use words. Put how that problem will
look when it is fixed on the top of the paper - that is where you are going.
Again, you can draw a picture or use words. Then cross out the street names on
your map and rename them with names of things you have to do in order to fix
your problem (get from where you are to where you want to be – like *Get a Job
Street* or *Go to Drug Treatment Street*
15. Look at your map. Find the first major intersection. If you went the wrong
way at that intersection, what would be doing? For example, the wrong turn
might be *hanging around with old friends*.
    (Any honest answer will do.)
16. Then with your wrong turn - think about what you might you see and hear that
would make you think that going down this street was OK rather than heading
toward your goal. How do people feel when they are heading down the wrong
street? What might be some of their thoughts?
    (Any honest answer will do.)

A Cognitive-Behavioral Framework for Sanction Implementation

Reprinted with permission of the American Correctional Association, Alexandria, Va.

Fry, R. (2002). A cognitive-behavioral framework for sanction implementation. *Corrections Today, 12,* 22-24.

Imagine you are driving along the interstate, maybe going to a conference on effective uses of cognitive-behavioral interventions in community corrections, and you glance up to see a police car's lights flashing in your mirror. You look at the speedometer and see that you are going 15 mph over the speed limit. You might say to yourself, "I'll bet this will cost me $100. I've just got to be more careful."

Imagine your surprise when instead of just getting a citation, the trooper handcuffs you and takes you to jail. When you find out that the standard penalty for 15 mph over the limit is 30 days, you think, "What is wrong with these people? Why are they making such a big deal out of this?"

Somewhere in this whole process, your thoughts switched from what you had done wrong to thoughts of how you were being victimized. You went from thinking about what you might be able to do to prevent it from happening again to minimizing your illegal behavior.

Now imagine what goes through you're the minds of your offenders when you sanction them. Do you think a mental process similar to this ever takes place in their minds? Throughout the middle of the past century, behavioral psychologists preached that the most effective sanctions were those that were swift, certain and severe. They proved it, too, by giving electric shocks to rats in special cages. But humans are not rats.

Nevertheless, sanctions that are delivered swiftly increase change in the desired direction more so than those delivered long after the incident occurs. Sanctions that are certain to be delivered are more likely to produce the desired change than those that are inconsistent or delayed. However, there is a point of diminishing returns when it comes to severity.

It might help to think of the effectiveness of sanctions as lying on a bell curve (See Appendix – Bell Curve). As the severity increases, so does change in attitude. At some point, though, at the top of the bell, increases in the severity of a sanction result in a decrease in the desired attitudinal change. If this were not so, everyone coming out of prison would go on to lead legal and stable lives, but this does not usually happen. At some point, a sanction becomes harsh enough that a person's thoughts change from what he or she believes they did wrong to how they are being punished more severely than is warranted.

According to Leon Festinger's *A Theory of Cognitive Dissonance*, the classic cognitive dissonance theory explanation for this is that:

> ... if one wanted to obtain private change in addition to mere public compliance, the best way to do this would be to offer just enough reward or punishment to elicit the overt compliance. If the reward or threat were too strong, only little dissonance would be created and one would not expect private change to follow as often.

Stricter sanctions tend to elicit greater public compliance, but only if the individual thinks he or she will get caught, and consequently, have to pay the penalty. Corrections has a responsibility to seek extrinsic compliance, but its overall goal should be intrinsic compliance. Offenders should freely choose to obey the law, even when they are no longer under supervision.

A person's sense of justice lies where the top of the bell curve rests. Pro-social people are more willing to accept what the law dictates as fair. Sure, everyone grumbles a little when they get caught doing something wrong — some grumble a lot. But most people accept their punishment and move on. They try to do better in the future.

People with more anti-social tendencies feel righteous indignation when they are sanctioned for wrongdoings (See Appendix – Locked Into Crime). Those feelings arise from a variety of beliefs that they use to explain away their illegal behavior. Studies by social learning theory pioneer Albert Bandura and colleagues outline how people can use mental tricks that allow them to justify their harmful behaviors (at least to themselves) and neutralize any bad feelings they may have been experiencing (See Appendix – Moral Disengagement). Habitual use of this type of moral disengagement allows a person to continue hurting others and not feel bad about doing so.

Since, unlike laboratory animals, people can excuse away their bad behavior; corrections must deal with offenders' belief systems as they are, not from where we want them to be. Therefore, if we want an effective framework for the implementation of sanctions, we should combine the swiftness and certainty of behavior therapy and the belief restructuring of cognitive therapy. In other words, we should use cognitive-behavioral interventions.

Where do most probation officers stand on this today? If you have a typical program, your probation officers give violators a string of warnings until finally following through with a punishment as the last straw. "If you keep getting positive urine tests, I'm taking you back to court." "If you miss one more appointment, you are going to jail." "You had better get a job soon or I'll stick you in the halfway house." This method is unswift, uncertain and unintense.

In all fairness to probation officers, effective intermediate sanctions are difficult to develop and enforce. Making a curfew more restrictive is not an effective punishment for someone who is not abiding by his or her curfew in the first place. Further, courts prefer not to deal with minor violations and they are anything but swift and certain anyway.

How can this be resolved? It will require a paradigm shift. The mission of community corrections is to protect the community from offenders committing further crimes and to promote their rehabilitation. Revocation and incarceration should be reserved only for those who re-offend or who, in the best judgment of the probation office, prosecutors and courts, have violated their supervision contracts in a pattern that indicates that they are an imminent threat to public safety.

Determining who has re-offended is usually pretty straightforward — an offender is arrested and convicted. On the other hand, determining if an offender has violated his or her supervision contracts in a pattern that indicates an imminent threat to public safety is less straightforward. Establishing violations is not the difficult part; what is difficult is deciding when there is clear and convincing evidence that a series of technical violations reveal that an offender will probably re-offend soon, and should be removed from the community before that happens.

As difficult as this is, we do it all the time, and we should continue to do it. The real challenge is determining what we should do about technical violations that do not rise to this level of imminent probable re-offense. What should we do with offenders who, if they do not change their ways, might constitute such a threat someday, but who currently do not and might not later if we find the right intervention?

The first step is to separate supervision management problems from criminogenic pathway behaviors. Supervision management problems make running a caseload difficult, but do not necessarily indicate that offenders are going to recidivate. For example, offenders may miss office visits, move without permission, skip treatment sessions, not pay restitution and change jobs without permission. These things are typically violations of their supervision contract and signs of irresponsible behavior, but they do not necessarily indicate that re-offending is imminent. Breaking the little rules does not mean a person is breaking the big rules.

Criminogenic pathway behaviors, on the other hand, indicate the presence of destabilizing factors that pave the way for criminal behavior. Positive urine tests, abandoning treatment, associating with old friends and long periods of unemployment with no signs of an effort to find work are some examples. While supervision management problems can probably be more easily tolerated, criminogenic pathway behaviors cannot. Each and every act of a criminogenic pathway violation must be dealt with swiftly, with certainty and with the right amount of severity if it is to be extinguished.

One possible approach is to file a violation complaint as soon as a criminogenic pathway violation becomes known. The complaint should be scheduled to be heard at the next available court date. Make it known to the offenders and their attorneys that unless you believe that an offender's behavior presents a serious risk warranting consideration for revocation, your recommendation will be three days in jail each and every time violation of this type occurs.

Will this work from a practical point of view? Maybe. If the hearings only last ten minutes, the court attendant who schedules court time will like this process and they should not last more than that if they go uncontested. If a complaint is contested, however, the hearing could easily be postponed to a later date when more time is available. Prosecutors will like this procedure if the complaint is not contested. If it is contested, however, they could recommend a stiffer sanction than what the probation officer recommends. The judges will like this process if it leads to fewer full-blown revocation hearings and if the parties work everything out beforehand. The defense attorneys will like this process because their clients will receive small sanctions without risking the wrath of the court and imprisonment for an easily established violation.

This would be swift. This would be as certain as anything in corrections is. There would be no dickering, no negotiations, and no deals. If you violate, this is what happens - period. It would be severe enough that offenders will not like it, but not so severe that they blame everyone else but themselves for their wrongdoings.

You might be thinking that the offender is getting off easy. Are 20 trips to jail at three days per trip getting off easier than a single trip for 60 days? Which would more likely change behavior? You might also be thinking that a person with a string of viola-tions does not deserve such consideration. He or she may not, but corrections' job is to protect the community and rehabilitate the offender. Whether an offender deserves it is not the issue. You might be thinking that other offenders will begin to break rules because they think that the punishments are not a big deal. I contend that they will think the opposite once they see that each and every time they break one of the major technical rules, they get penalized.

If we want to change attitudes, if we want to make more effective use of our resources, if we want to make our communities safer, we need to think in ways different from what we have in the past. Is this approach different? Yes. Will it work? Maybe. At least it has support from some established theories behind it. Is it worth a try? You can be the judge of that, but I say yes.

References:

Andrews, D. and J. Bonta. 1998. The psychology of criminal conduct. Cincinnati: Anderson Publishing.

Bandura, A., C. Barbaranelli, G.V. Caprara and C. Pastorelli. 1996. Mechanisms of moral disengagement in the exercise of moral agency. Journal of Personality and Social Psychology, 71:364-374.

Festinger. L 1957. A theory of cognitive dissonance. Stanford: Stanford University Press.

Three Pathways to Criminal Behavior

Fry, R. (2007). Three pathways to criminal behavior. *Offender Programs Report, 11:1*, 1-14.

The last time I had my eyes examined, the optometrist (knowing I was a probation officer) asked me what caused people to become criminals. Was it alcohol and drugs or bad parenting? I thought for a second and replied with a question of my own. What is the cause of eye problems? He looked puzzled at first and then replied that there is no single cause for eye problems. There are many different causes. Each patient must be examined and treated according to whatever is specifically wrong with their eyes. I then replied that the same was true for crime.

NATURAL EMPATHY

Before we delve into criminal behavior, let me first tell you a story. Imagine that it is a beautiful spring day. The sun is shining and the grass is turning green again. As you walk down the street, you see a young boy, maybe eight or nine years old. He is holding his little sister's hand. They are standing near an intersection. You can tell that he is explaining to her that she needs to always look both ways before crossing the street. Once it appears safe, they begin to cross the road. Suddenly, a car speeds out of nowhere and hits them both. They are killed instantly.

Even though this story is just so many words on paper, it still tears at your heart. Imagine the depth of feelings you might experience if you had actually witnessed such a tragic event. Empathy, compassion and altruism are natural parts of the human psyche

(McGuire and Troisi, 1998; Pinker, 1997). We feel how others feel and their pain moves us to want to help.

Empathy and compassion also serve as a pre-emptive self-restraining mechanism that prevents us from harming others. Normally, when a person is tempted to hurt someone, they experience the painful consequences in their mind first and then reject that course of action (Bandura, Barbaranelli, Caprara and Pastorelli, 1996).

Offenders are people whose natural empathy and compassion has failed to restrain their behavior for some reason. They have harmed others and are at risk of doing so again. We can understand this failure better if we separate criminal behavior into three different categories: psychopathy, dysreasoning and moral disengagement (See Appendix – Moral Disengagement). Knowing which category an offender falls into will help us assess his problems and provide services according to what is specifically wrong with his behavior.

PSYCHOPAHTY

One of the three categories of criminal behavior is psychopathy. Psychopaths are people whose brains are wired in such a ways that they do not easily experience empathy, if at all (Damasio 1994). Intellectually they know when others are suffering, but they do not feel it. They lack the natural self-restraining mechanism provided by compassion. This leaves them free to satisfy their wants and needs regardless of the consequences to others (Hare, 1993). They are indifferent to the pain they cause others.

What is to be done with psychopaths?

Don Andrews, one of the authors of the Level of Service Inventory – Revised (LSI-R) states that, "We have no evidence in the literature that intensive human services

with the highest risk, extremely egocentric, offenders will reduce re-offending (1996)."
Furthermore, treatment may even make them worse (Hare, 1993). On the other hand there
is evidence that intensive security-type supervision for higher-risk offenders reduces
recidivism (Latessa, 2004).

Rehabilitation efforts for psychopaths are not warranted. Instead the objective
should be increasing public safety through closer supervision and incarceration.

DYSREASONING

Another group of offenders do not intend to harm others, but continue to do so
nevertheless. A lack of empathy is not the problem – it is a lack of the knowledge, skills
and resources to control their problem behavior. Their pre-emptive self-restraining
mechanism is sidetracked and their capacity to anticipate the harmful consequences of
their behavior is subsequently compromised. They end up hurting themselves and others.
I call this sidetracking process dysreasoning.

Impulsivity

Some people are prone to impulsivity; they jump into action before they think
things through. People with this temperament are not only impulsive, but trust their
impulses and feel frustrated if they are restrained from acting on them, even if this has
been a source of problems for them in the past (Keirsey, 1998).

In addition, people under stress tend to be impulsive, regardless of their
temperament (Tice, Bratslavsky and Baumeister, 2001). When a person is stressed out,
they cannot think clearly and are driven more by how they feel than by reason.

Clouded Judgment

Clouded judgment and moods also result in dysreasoning (Epstein and Brodsky, 1993). Rather than seeking confirming evidence for their interpretation of events, people under the influence of clouded judgment just feel confident that they know what is going on. Rather than formulating a variety of choices, they only think of options that are consistent with their current state of emotions. Their moods bias their decision-making in ways that often cause them problems.

Self-defeating Beliefs

Another source of dysreasoning is self-defeating beliefs (Ellis and Harper, 1961; Beck, 1995). Self-defeating beliefs limit a person's thinking by providing irrational, inflexible responses to life's situations, instead of developing effective solutions in an ever-changing environment (See Appendix – REBT). Rather than being resilient and creative, people guided by self-defeating beliefs do things a certain way every time, whether that way is useful or not.

Palliative Relief

Sometime people seek palliative relief rather than take effective action (Epstein and Brodsky, 1993; Tice, Bratslavsky and Baumeister, 2001). They do something that makes them feel good, at least temporarily, but that does not address the source of their problems. They overeat, gamble, shop, or use alcohol and other drugs. They may do something that makes them feel dominant and powerful. They kick the dog or yell at the kids. They may feel better, but their problems generally get worse.

Alcohol and Other Drugs

Alcohol and other drugs can also lead to a dysreasoning by altering brain functions (Alcohol and Cognition, 1989; Alcohol-Related Impairment, 1994). While alcohol and other intoxicating drugs affect the whole brain, they tend to diminish higher cognitive functions quicker and to a greater extent than they do lower brain functions (Fishman, 1986). People do things under the influence that they would not do if they were sober.

Mental Disorders

Mental disorders can also be a cause of dysreasoning. They can compromise a person's information processing and other functional capacities (McGuire and Troisi, 1998). People with active disorders may not have the capacity to make rational decisions and in that sense their decisions can be viewed an irresistible compulsions.

What is to be done about dysreasoning?

If an offender is not ready to make changes, motivational enhancement (such as motivational interviewing) should be the first course of action (Miller and Rollnick, 1991; Prochaska, Norcross, DiClemente, 1994) (See Appendix – Motivational Interviewing). The objective is to help the offender recognize his role in his problems and recognize his role in the solutions.

When an offender is treatment ready, the objective becomes to restructure the beliefs that make the self-defeating behavior seem acceptable to the offender. He needs to develop the knowledge, skills and resources (including medication, if needed) necessary to change his problem behavior.

MORAL DISENGAGEMENT

People who harm others are at a crossroads. They feel bad when their behavior is inconsistent with their values. These bad feelings are called cognitive dissonance (Festinger, 1957). They can rid themselves of the bad feelings by changing their self-defeating behaviors or by changing their beliefs and values in ways that allows them to maintain a positive self-image.

If they change their harmful behavior, things improve. However, if they take the other path, they develop beliefs that justify the harm they have done (See Appendix – Moral Disengagement). With selective attention, reinforcing thoughts and associating with like-minded people, they excuse away their bad behavior. As their empathy and compassion decreases, their willingness to commit new crimes increases (Bandura, Barbaranelli, Caprara and Pastorelli, 1996).

Furthermore, the dynamics of moral disengagement can lock them into a pattern of progressively antisocial behaviors (See Appendix – Locked Into Crime). If an offender commits a crime and escapes punishment, he sees himself as superior to others and gives himself a license to do whatever he wants.

If he gets caught and punished, his thoughts turn to avoiding getting caught next time, not changing his troublesome behavior. He associates the punishment with the punisher, not with what he has done. He believes that he is the victim of unfair treatment and feels righteous indignation. Even in losing, he sees himself as superior to others and gives himself a license to do whatever he wants.

What is to be done about moral disengagement?

Again, if motivation is an issue, it must be dealt with first. Then, in addition to dealing with dysreasoning (if there is any), the offender needs to realize that the beliefs that allow him to hurt others without feeling bad are the source of his own problems (and the problems he is causing others). The objective is to restructure the beliefs that block natural empathy and to increase his awareness of the true width and depth of the harm caused by his criminal acts.

CONCLUSION

The psychology of criminal behavior is complex, but it is not a mystery. By focusing on psychopathy, dysreasoning or moral disengagement, corrections will have the perspective necessary to protect the community and help offenders change. I do not think we need to have our eyes examined to clearly see the advantages of looking at criminal behavior this way.

References:

Alcohol and cognition. (1989). *National Institute on Alcohol Abuse and Alcoholism, 4.* [Online] Available: http://www.niaaa.nih.gov/publications/aa04.htm. [2003, April 7].

Alcohol-related impairment. (1994). *National Institute on Alcohol Abuse and Alcoholism, 25,* [Online] Available: http://www.niaaa.nih.gov/publications/aa25.htm. [2003, April 7].

Andrews, D. (Narrator) (1996). *Summary of the LSI-R: Training video series. Vol. I: Theoretical rationale* [Videotape]. (Available from Multi-Health systems, Inc., 908 Niagara Falls Blvd., North Tonawanda, NY 14120)

Bandura, A., Barbaranelli, C., Caprara, G. V., Pastorelli, C. (1996). Mechanisms of moral disengagement in the exercise of moral agency. *Journal of Personality and Social Psychology, 71,* 364-374.

Beck, J. (1995). *Cognitive therapy: Basics and beyond.* New York: Guilford Press.

Damasio, A. (1994). *Descartes' error: Emotion, reason, and the human brain.* New York: Avon Books.

Ellis, A., Harper, R. (1961). *A guide to rational living.* Hollywood, CA: Wilshire Book Company.

Festinger, L. (1957). *A theory of cognitive dissonance.* Stanford: Stanford University Press.

Fishman, R. (1986). *The encyclopedia of psychoactive drugs.* New York: Chelsea House.

Hare, R. (1993). *Without conscience: The disturbing world of the psychopaths among us.* New York: Guilford Press

Keirsey, D. (1998). *Please understand me II: Temperament character intelligence.* Del Mar, CA.: Prometheus Nemesis.

Latessa, E. (2004). Understanding the risk principle: How and why correctional interventions can harm low risk offenders. *Topics in Community Corrections – 2004.*

McGuire, M., Troisi, A. (1998). *Darwinian psychiatry.* New York: Oxford University Press.

Miller, W., Rollnick, S. (1991). *Motivational Interviewing: Preparing people to change addictive behavior.* New York: Gilford Press.

Pinker, S. (1997). *How the mind works.* New York: W. W. Norton and Co.

Prochaska, J., Norcross, J., DiClemente, C. (1994). *Changing for good.* New York: William Morrow and company.

Tice, M., Bratslavsky, E., Baumeister, R. (2001) Emotional distress regulation takes precedence over impulse control: If you feel bad, do it. *Journal of Personality and Social Psychology, 80,* 53-67.

Community Corrections' Core Mission

Reprinted with permission of the American Correctional Association, Alexandria, Va.

Fry, R. (2007). Community corrections' Core Mission. *Corrections Today*. 69:2, 14.

Most people in community corrections would probably agree that our core mission is to provide the maximum opportunity for the rehabilitation of offenders without compromising community safety in the process. The primary method we use to carry out this mission is to set up and enforce rules in the form of supervision agreements.

The ultimate reward for following the rules is that an offender does not have to go to prison. Additionally, there may be secondary rewards along the way such as reduced restrictions and early discharge. The ultimate punishment for violating the rules is revocation and incarceration.

The subtle belief behind this "supervision by rules" approach is that the people under our care will not make the desired changes without coercive pressures on our part. It is true that rules without sanctions are just suggestions and suggestions are seldom sufficient to motivate significant change. However, operating this way creates certain dynamics that move us away from our core mission and guarantees the failure of many of the offenders who need our efforts the most.

It is clearly our job to recommend the revocation of offenders whose violations present a clear and imminent threat to public safety, but what should we do about violations that do not rise to that level? Surely prison is not a proper sanction for a missed office visit or for being fired. For these we typically use intermediate sanctions; something less severe, but sufficient to "get their attention." We make them report more often, impose curfews, add extra community service or put them in jail for the weekend.

What if that does not work? What if they continue to miss visits? We make the sanctions progressive. If one weekend in jail does not teach them that we mean business, maybe a whole week will. If a whole week does not work, maybe sixty days. Before we know it, we have tried every sanction in our arsenal and revocation is all we have left. Unfortunately, the creditability of doing business this way demands it – regardless of our core mission.

Seldom do we revoke offenders because the possibility of rehabilitation is null or because they are an increased danger to the community. More often we revoke offenders because we cannot get them to do what we tell them to do.

Offenders who come to us already possessing the knowledge, skills and resources to lead a legal and stable lifestyle often succeed – even without our help. Offenders who do not have this ability in place will not develop them just because we threaten them with imprisonment. It is our job to go beyond this and help them learn how to manage emotions, problem solve, refute irrational beliefs, manage time, recognize and be prepared for risky situations, deal with cravings and keep a job. This takes time and effort on an offender's part and on our part as well.

Granted, most offenders are not initially motivated to learn these things. Their resistance, however, comes from ignorance – in many ways self-inflicted. They do not recognize and accept their role in their problems and they do not recognize and accept their role in the solutions. Nevertheless, if we make it our job, most of this ignorance can be dissolved by using techniques such as motivational interviewing and discovery/experiential based groups (See Appendix – Motivational Interviewing).

If we rely exclusively on progressive intermediate sanctions, the most we can expect to accomplish is that some offenders will postpone their troublesome behaviors until they get off of supervision. What we are more likely to see is that they try to find ways of doing what they want without getting caught. It becomes a two way "us against them" struggle with everyone losing.

Intermediate non-progressive sanctions coupled with motivation enhancement help offenders reach the conclusion that the things we want them to learn are in their best interest; that knowing these things will help them get the things they truly want without creating more problems for themselves and those around them. Rather than an "us against them" struggle it becomes a collaborative effort that makes everyone's lives better.

Radical Responsivity

Reprinted with permission of the American Correctional Association, Alexandria, Va.

Fry, R. (2006). Radical responsivity. *Corrections Today. 68:7,* 20.

This article was selected by the American Corrections Association as one of its major articles in its *Corrections Today* Index for 2007.

Imagine you just got an email from your boss. You were ordered to attend a special training because of something you did wrong earlier in the year. If that were not bad enough, you have to do it on your own time and at your own expense. How would you feel?

Now think about the offenders you order to treatment. How might they feel? You might be thinking right now, "Yes, but what they did was really wrong – they really do need to make changes. My boss, on the other hand, is just going overboard." Regardless of whether that is all true or not, it does point out that resistance is a very human thing.

What are we to think about offender resistance? "They don't want to change." "They are incapable of changing." "They are lazy." "If they resist, they should go to prison." Radical Responsivity tells us to think something altogether different.

Responsivity, if you remember, is one of the three main principles for changing criminal behavior put forth by Don Andrews and James Bonta – the developers of the Level of Service Inventory. The other two are the risk principle and the needs principle.

Responsivity means that in order to enhance the change process, you should match style and mode of service to the learning styles and motivational levels of the population served. Radical Responsivity says that if a person does not successfully complete a program - they did not fail, you failed to match them to a program in which they could succeed.

That is a serious accusation. Do I believe it? Yes. Well sort of. Some offenders lack the cognitive capacity for circumspection and foresight. They just cannot "get it", regardless of what we offer them or how we offer it. However, they represent only a small percentage of the people we work with.

Other offenders do not particularly like the legal problems they find themselves in, but accept them as being the price they have to pay for doing what they want to do. Therefore, responsivity is not relevant when working with them. However, I would guess that these offenders are few and far between as well. More likely, a large percentage of people who think this way probably have just given up trying to change. It is a lack of confidence and not incorrigibility.

Excluding these two groups (and the always handy defense - "I don't have enough resources to do all of the things I should be doing."), I am a Radical Responsivitist. However, we still have not addressed what we should think about offender resistance? My opinion is that they are resistant because they "believe" that what we are trying to do for them is:

> **Not Relevant** - the treatment outcome is not something they value. For example, "I like getting high. It's not a problem for me."
>
> **Not Necessary** - they have already accomplished the treatment outcome. For example, "I used to have a problem, but not anymore."
>
> **Not a Priority** – the treatment outcome is a lower priority than the other things they are currently spending their time, resources and energy on. For example, "My job is more important than these classes."
>
> **Worthless** - the treatment program will not help them reach a valued outcome. For example, "This class is just plain stupid. It has nothing to do with what's going on in my life."

Leery - the treatment environment will not be comfortable (free from embarrassment, boredom, conflict, etc.)? For example, "I don't want to go. What if they ask me to read something?"

Their resistance-creating beliefs may be correct or incorrect and we have an obligation to not just assume that their resistance is without cause. However, most resistive offenders do not feel they need to change because they do not see themselves as the source of their problems and do not see themselves as the source of the solutions. Treatment approaches such as Bill Miller and Steve Rollnick's Motivational Interviewing (along with short-term intermediate sanctions) are the way to deal with treatment resistance, not prison (See Appendix – Motivational Interviewing). Motivational enhancement is as legitimate of a goal for corrections as is helping offenders develop the knowledge, skills and resources to end their problematic behaviors. Offenders should be revoked if they pose an immediate threat to the community, not when they are resistive to treatment.

References:

Andrews, D., Bonta, J. (1998). *The psychology of criminal conduct.* (2nd. ed.). Cincinnati: Anderson Publishing.

Miller, W., Rollnick, S. (2002). *Motivational interviewing: Preparing people for change. (2nd ed.).* New York: Gilford Press.